A MURDER OF CRONES

A COLLECTION

THE
MOSTLY POETS

Louie Adell
Elizabeth Bartel
Vera Jensen
Marieluisa Auterson
Sharon Tilton Urdahl
Katherine Kane
Jan Bush
Judith Heron

FIRST EDITION 2007

Ptarmigan Press
Canada

First edition – March 2007

Library and Archives Canada Cataloguing in Publication

A murder of crones : a collection : Louie Adell, Elizabeth Bartel, Vera Jensen, Marieluisa Auterson, Sharon Tilton Urdahl, Katherine Kane, Jan Bush, Judith Heron / The Mostly Poets.

Poems.
ISBN 978-0-919537-69-9

1. Canadian poetry (English)--Women authors. 2. Canadian poetry (English)--21st century. I. Mostly Poets (Group)

PS8283.F3M87 2007   C811'.60809287   C2007-901201-9

Cover art- original pastel "Portrait" ©
Copyright Sharon Tilton Urdahl
Front and back cover- design,
Book layout and design - Sharon Tilton Urdahl

Black and white Photo-Crow ©
Copyright -Judith Heron

Set in Bookman ITC LT Bt type
Printed on Kafka and recycled trees
Printed and bound in Canada

Publisher – Ptarmigan Press
1372 – 16th Avenue
Campbell River, B.C.
Canada V9W 2E1

DEDICATION

*To poets and readers
all lovers of words
whose eyes and hands
this book will grace.*

ACKNOWLEDGEMENTS

Members of the "Mostly Poets" thank and acknowledge the following people and groups for their encouragement and support.

Sharon Niscak for being liaison between "Mostly Poets" and The League of Canadian Poets, whose funding for our poetry readings in past years, has enabled us to publish *A Murder of Crones –A Collection*, our first group volume of poetry.

A sincere thank you and much appreciation to Sheila Munro and Ed Varney for making time in their own busy schedules to review and comment on *A Murder of Crones*.

Special thanks to the Muir Gallery, and Comox Valley Art Gallery in Courtenay, as well as Pearl Ellis Gallery in Comox for their ongoing support of the literary arts by providing space for poetry to be both read and appreciated.

A very special thank you to all fellow poets and listeners who attend readings and open microphone events hosted by the "Mostly Poets." Thank you to all readers who support the literary arts, especially the "revival of poetry," with your purchase of this book, *A Murder of Crones –A Collection*.

Acknowledgement and gratitude to the editing committee for their diligence and care: Judith Heron, Vera Jensen, Katherine Kane and Sharon Tilton Urdahl.

Heartfelt thanks to families and friends who encourage, listen, support and rarely complain when we disappear for hours, days or weeks, alone...to write.

PREFACE

The Mostly Poets' critique group began with first three, then four members, and has over the years, grown to a close gathering of eight very diverse women. We are poets who have become close friends, dedicated to writing personal poetry and encouraging each other's creativity. Every other week we meet to both give and receive respectful, honest critique.

From those meetings the idea of publishing a book of our poetry evolved...it has taken over a year of planning to bring the publication to completion. You now hold in your hands, an honest labour of love, a product of many long hours of writing, reading, editing, deleting and still more editing, our truths, souls, and lives, literally becoming an open book.

Our ages, number of members and wry sense of humour, determined that we title our publication, *A Murder of Crones, A Collection*, a play on words...the interpretation hopefully made obvious to readers by a crow seen at the end of each poet's section, and the small feather floating between poems. The order of poets as presented in the book, was chosen in our group's usual, democratic way...by draw.

Sharon Tilton Urdahl

INTRODUCTION

A Murder of Crones

In this delightful poetry collection, eight talented and exceptional women, all members of the Comox Valley's "Mostly Poets" group, share their life experience; the insight, wisdom and compassion that has come to them over the years. Whether it's the small epiphanies that arise from observations of the natural world, the memories of days long past, or the spiritual meditations on the soul's desires, all are represented here in these distinctive and original voices.

Very often it is the small things that count; a wisp of silver hair released into the wind, a bunch of basil left on a chair outside, a mother bringing in clothes from the line on a winter's day. There are birds and flowers, walks along the Comox estuary, November skies, moments opening up onto something larger, something magical.

There are also the commentaries on aging and loss, whether it's the tenderness of a daughter describing her mother's Alzheimers, the courage of a woman who escapes to an imaginary world while under the radiation machine, the poignancy of another who sees her grandchildren moving into the future without her, or the rueful humour of a woman who refuses to recognize the old face in the mirror. These women celebrate life, but they do not shy away from painful subjects, and are able to confront them head-on, without lapsing into cliché or sentimentality. In age there may be sadness and loss, but there is also the freedom that comes from letting go; the detachment and moments of transformation that are harder to find in youth.

One of the collection's contributors likens a poem to "*an interlude, a pause like breath held between inhaling and exhaling*" which made me think of the way true meditation happens in that brief moment between one thought and the next, when some deeper awareness opens up for us. Reading *A Murder of Crones* reminded me that it is often in those moments, whether it's in meditation or in reading a poem that we surrender to the moment and are most fully alive.

Sheila Munro
Author of the best selling book,
Lives of Mothers & Daughters:
Growing Up with Alice Munro

Mostly Poets
eight women
sharing a love of poetry

diverse in writing
as we are in our lives
ages span forty years

different backgrounds
life experiences
revealed in verse

we bring poems
dishes of food
bonds of friendship

eight women
sharing a love of writing
poetry...mostly

By Katherine Kane

TABLE OF CONTENTS

Louie Adell
Pages 1 - 17

Elizabeth Bartel
Pages 19 – 35

Vera Jensen
Pages 37 – 53

Marieluisa Auterson
Pages 55 – 71

Sharon Tilton Urdahl
Pages 73 – 89

Katherine Kane
Pages 91 - 107

Jan Bush
Pages 109 – 125

Judith Heron
Pages 127 – 143

Louie Adell was born and raised in the USA, and has been writing poetry for over thirty years. While in her twenties she studied poetry at Naropa Institute with, as she says *"some of the Beat Generation's finest drunks."*

Louie is a resident of Black Creek on Vancouver Island, B.C., where she and Randy share their lives with her eighty-six year-old mother, who has Alzheimers. They also have four sheep and two dogs. Louie enjoys living on their land where she gathers, cans and freezes the produce from Randy's huge garden.

Many of Louie's poems are about the land and her family. In her own words she states, *"I hope that my poetry captures some of the joy and fun of life: either that or the pain and suffering. Give me something with emotion,"* she says. *"I hope you enjoy my poems."*

She has had poems published in the US and Mexico, belongs to several "peer poetry" groups and has been a member of the "Mostly Poets" critique group for three years. Louie has participated in many open microphone events as a reader, but also enjoys organizing and being a host/emcee.

1

TABLE OF CONTENTS

Chanukah Derailed — 3

Yiddisha Lullaby — 4

Home — 5

Randy And Mom — 6

This Ever Fading — 6

My Father's Pumpkin Pie — 7

Winter Approaches — 8

Edible Parts — 8

Simply — 10

Apparitions — 10

Ode To A Beautiful — 11

I Will Weave — 12

The T.V. — 14

The Pity Of It All — 15

Chemainus — 16

Requiem For A Childhood Friendship — 17

CHANUKAH DERAILED

My father and Randy are
in the Emergency Room
my father's second fall in three days.
As I cook the latkes
my mother asks the same question
five times in a row
each thinly separated
by a minute or less.
I ask her to leave the kitchen...

But preparing latkes alone is absurd
no enthusiastic crowd hovering
near the stove
eating them as fast as I can cook them
fighting over the last one hot off the pan.
No one stealing a latke only
three-quarters done
when my back is turned.
I only know that one has been taken
when I see them blowing on their fingers
or looking like a fish with an
"O" shaped mouth
and making funny noises
as they try to suck in enough air
to cool the hot grease.

My mother comes back in.
To my question
   "Would you like a hot latke? "
she answers
   "Maybe-aybe"
and turns to the door
   "I have this on one lock,
   shouldn't I double lock it?"
She bends and the lock clicks loudly.

She turns and heads into the dining room
to see if there are any blinds
that need to be pulled down
or lights to be turned off
or drapes to be closed
or doors to be checked
her circular vigil throughout the house...

YIDDISHA LULLABY

He slowly stroked my hair
as he sang in a soft monotone,
a song his mother had sung to him
when he lived in a Bronx flat
back when there was a farm
at the end of the street
and WWI was raging.

Now there is only the sadness
of an old man
and a song my father can no longer sing.

Only sound bites of tenderness
seep through my erected wall
of the day-to-day busyness
in being my parents' caregiver.
Doctor calls, missing teeth and
malfunctioning hearing aids.
Blood levels, food shopping and laundry.
Wheel chairs, pill minders and urinals.

What I really want to do
is slow down and hear the song
but what I do
is shield myself from the song.

HOME

I want to feel
the silver of the new moon
with your arms wrapped around me
clouds breezing through
and the frogs burping
down in the pond.

I don't want to hear the musical-mechanical
hum-clank of the excavator
as it rips the large
second growth Douglas firs
from the skin of the Earth
down where the creek joins the ocean
where I stood with my dog
and screamed silently
    It was perfect.
    It used to be green.

I never thought I'd
once again be standing on this shore
and be calling it mine.

I always knew that one day
I'd be selling my childhood home
and cutting all ties to upstate New York
but was able to put it off
each year my father lived.
Each year a reprieve.

I have always wanted to travel
to move amongst geography
not be saddled with one country
one country only
but I never had invented
or invited
goodbye.

RANDY AND MOM
(Solstice 2003)

A tall person holding
the hand of a much shorter person
dwarfed by cathedral-tall trees.
He, dressed in grey and black
she, in a bright pink coat and red hat
easier to see if she wanders off.
They walk past waist-high ferns and
thick slabs of soft moss which hang off trees
or sit on rocks in almost
every shade of yellow-green.
She looks up at him, smiles
and as a five year old in an aged body
points out everything she sees.
A few long rays of sun
shaft through the trees
the air moist like spring.

THIS EVER FADING

The names are on the bottom
of each family photo
to ward off the questions
my mom will ask again and again
in this fragmented
slow fall of her life.

Randy and I, her caregivers
are in the middle of her fading memory.
Others from her past are on the fringes
like a halo of light circling.
Mostly the shapes are ill-lit
out of focus, vague....
but sometimes the light is bright.

MY FATHER'S PUMPKIN PIE

I remember your pumpkin pie
you made the worst pumpkin pie...
it was only partially cooked
but I actually liked it
it had lots of pumpkin
and not too sweet
since you were frugal with sugar.
Neighbours started one upmanships
of awful cooking by mentioning your pie.
I remained silent
a twinkle in my eye...
they'd never tasted your Western Omelettes
that had half eaten salads thrown in...

I remember you
like it was yesterday
not two years ago.

I remember winter snow...
you'd be wearing countless layers
like one big snowman
so cuddly to hug...

I remember dishes of ice cream at 7:30...
after eating we'd rinse the bowls
place them next to the sink
the dull florescent light
the tinny hum of the refrigerator
classical music filtering in
from the radio on the headboard
above your bed
down the long narrow hall...

I remember you...
how could I ever forget.

WINTER APPROACHES

Wrap me in your warm arms
I wish to forget this sadness
let me add it to the fire
a heavy log I have carried
and clung to
not bellying up to the task
of burial
or acceptance.

While birds twitter on the feeder
I am left with dust, boot marks
back at square one...
with the smell of sorrow
held too long in the warp of my clothes.

EDIBLE PARTS

Ah food and you...
will it be piles of steaming vegetables
so bare that nothing lies
between me and you and
plates of beets, squash, kale and broccoli...
their reds, oranges and greens
beautiful and stark in their simplicity...
layered in their beetness, squashness
high in sugar
carbs fill up my pores
as once again you feed me.

Or is it lasagne
with our own leeks, garlic, tomatoes and herbs
for the next day
the following day
and the day after that?

It is hard to know where all the liquid went
we stared at one boiling soupy mess
in the morning the noodles
had soaked it all up.

The freezer is full...
trying to get to the stewed tomatoes
which are buried below the
two pound chunks of applesauce
berries and more berries
takes gloves, boxes
and a pitchfork
to hold up the corner of the heavy lid...
and fortitude...
after fifteen minutes of swearing
I have a wrenched back
and enough tomato sauce for this week
and next.

We will be eating squash, leeks, potatoes
and beets
when the berries, tomatoes and salad
fresh from the garden
are gone.
All winter we will dine on the four staples
from your garden.

We do not bypass the produce aisle
but tread lightly wishing to remain faithful
to the boxes of veggies at home.
We will buy salad fixings
but the staples will be
squash, leeks, potatoes and beets
until the sprouts of Spring.

SIMPLY

"May I have a simple form, please?"
To simply sit under the sun
as it soaks into my face and hair
my hair becoming darker and darker
with its absorbed heat.
To simply roll over on my back and look
at the big sky
and watch the clouds drift
take shapes
transform and migrate.
To simply eat from one bowl
my whole meal in that bowl
as I sit looking out on trees
and wind and stream
me and my bowl
becoming part of the woods
simply part of the woods.

APPARITIONS

Ghosts of Falls past
are peering around the corner
waiting for Summer to shed her body.
They whisper veiled warnings
pointing out each nuance of weakening.
We cheer her rallied strength
even as morning temperatures plunge
and we scramble to find
the hiding place of sweaters...
even as dark comes early
and constellations reappear before bedtime.
Even as the basil gets brown tips
we still put on tank tops
hoping we will be hot enough to wear them.

The days are glorious with sun
we sigh as crickets sing and dahlias bloom...
yet the calendar advances
and we know that November means rain.
The ghosts just fold their leafy arms
gloat and click their tongues
while rocking on their heels.
They wait as we frolic.

ODE TO A BEAUTIFUL

Ode to a beautiful
you big buck, you.
You stand there
nibbling on the tall grass,
long pink tongue lapping
up the sweet juice,
wondering
what the fuss is all about.
Well,
let me tell you
you are big
and beautiful
antlers tall and wide
five points on a side.
You walk
regally
head back
rack high.

I WILL WEAVE

Once again
I whine
as I walk warily
walloped by words
swirling in disfiguring speech
that echoes in the silence
of figuring it out.

Once again
I will weave
the threadbare smile
of coming out from under.
I will grovel if I must
but I will not be shamed.

Once again
I will weave
my way out of chaos
to create some sort of coherence...
I sift through words
tangled.

Once again
I will weave
the wary smile
of wine that is acrid
the twisted mouth
revamping expectations
erasing ingredients.

Once again
I will weave
my way to you
thank goodness you can
lend a hand.
that beautiful long hand of you...
crossing the creek
the ditch
the quicksand
of me
of words
of...

Once again
I will weave
you home.
You are wrong but
you are right.
Just come home to me...
one piece
whole
smiling
I will let you in.

THE T.V.

Given to us by my parents
it sits on top of the dresser
opposite the head of the bed
god-like.
Instead it serves
as a clothes-horse
dirty socks, pants, washcloths
hung over its side
one antenna is only partially up
a hook for Randy's nursing smock
stethoscope.

It feels well rested
old but
not forlorn.
When we do turn it on
it warms up slowly...
works on two out of four channels
at certain times.
It turns off
quickly, easily
becoming mirror-like
the glass reflecting.
It is then that I like to look at it.

THE PITY OF IT ALL

A young man
shoulder length dark curls
thin and tall
is playing with his car radio...
adjusting the volume upwards.
I sneak glances
trying not to show
that I am being drawn in.
The song breathes...
*"I feel like making love
but I can't make love to you."*

If I had the courage
I would face him
say something small like
"That's a nice song,"
and watch him blush.
Then I'd say...
"Goodbye."

I was afraid he would see
an older woman showing
her sexuality.
So I covered it up.
Didn't chance any contact.
Ran away...
smouldering.

CHEMAINUS

75-year-old Japanese man
sitting on the dock at low tide
sun baking a thick creosote perfume
into the still air.
Next to him is a paint peeling
seam split, rotting boat
its deck with various tools
and pieces of planking on sawhorses.
He's talking about the old days
fishing.
He and his father knew
the whole Inland Passage
without charts.
Forced to Ontario during the war
he returned to fish.
A bachelor
never married because
   *"What woman would want
      this unsettled life?"*
To now sit here
smiling
on the dock in Chemainus
at low tide
soaking up the sun.

REQUIEM FOR A CHILDHOOD FRIENDSHIP

Requiem for the green moon of youth
the bright ribbons of utter joy
burning in a narrow swath of time.
Oh to be a fool
in their loving embrace once more.

Tornados of foolishness
doorway to my soul
cut to ribbons
as the moon burns
my green memory of you.

A taut ribbon
still binds us.
I look back
its gauzy fabric fraying.

As the moon burns the waning hours of night
I must cut the fool green ribbon
that binds you to me.

Like a tornado
I cut
and burn.

Louie Adell

Elizabeth Bartel lives with her husband on Vancouver Island between the mountains and the sea, but has one foot firmly planted in the prairie soil of her childhood. She writes from the richness of her cultural heritage that celebrates the lives of ordinary people by showing them to be much more than that. Her poems span many years and as she takes the reader on a journey of life and death, laughter and tears, she vividly reflects upon her personal life from youth to present day.

Her poetry and short stories have been published in various literary magazines. Her first novel, *Even Such is Time*, was published in 2002. Elizabeth was a co-founder of the "Mostly Poets," a Comox Valley group of women poets. She now lives in Nanaimo, but remains an enthusiastic participant in group critiques and readings.

Besides her commitment to "Mostly Poets," Elizabeth is currently writing her memoirs and a novel based on the life of her grandfather, who came to Canada as a boy of nine and lived to be one hundred and two.

She devotes her time between her family, which includes several children, grandchildren, great-grandchildren and her love of writing.

19

TABLE OF CONTENTS

Along The Tracks	21
Joy	22
Flowers Don't Care	23
Swallows	23
Spring Wedding	24
Walking On The Estuary Path	25
Swimming	26
Better Not To Think	27
Grief	28
I Would Rather Horses	29
Slippers	30
Lisa At The Pool	31
After The Rain	32
Lament	33
Gratitude	34
One Hand Clapping	35

ALONG THE TRACKS

Mornings I walk
along the railroad track,
stop and listen
to trills and chirring, long flute-like notes
moving up and down the scale
like sailors whistling.

Suddenly a spruce bough sways
with the blur and
flutter of unseen wings.

Songbirds flown
from unimaginable distances.
Bits of flesh and feather with
glistening eyes
tiny beating hearts
survivors of wind storms and
endless miles of winter.

Now clothed in spring finery
they frisk about, comparing notes
in bird chatter.
They know what they know and are
not about to share their secrets.

And I thought
today I would hear only
the rusty cawing
of self-important crows.

JOY

Happiness:
a state of mind
that can be chosen.
But joy comes from another place.
It is that otherworldly thing
which sometimes yearns
in the heart of grief.

Joy
cannot be controlled,
manipulated
or bargained away.
Joy is only itself
which comes and goes
at the Spirit's bidding.

A gift.
A sighting of angels.
A taste of Heaven.
Joy swells the heart
to bring
a gush of hot tears
at the wonder of it all.

FLOWERS DON'T CARE

Flowers don't care how long they live.
They do all the wrong things,
scent the thoughtless air
spend their passions, hold back nothing.

Flowers just bloom and bloom
their petals drop without a sound.
When I go out to talk to them
I wish they could reply.

The roses round the fountain
only blush a deeper pink,
hang their heads like bashful children
not knowing how beautiful they are.

SWALLOWS

I bow my head
to the splendour of the morning sun.
Then, obeisance made,
I drape one corner of a laundered sheet
over my shoulder like royalty,
pin it to the clothesline
still strung with crystal beads of dew
that vanish at a touch.

Nearby a pair of love-sick swallows
chirp and flutter, about to nest
around the chimney.
By summer, we'll hear the cheep
of fledglings
as tell-tale wisps of straw
float above the deck,
well spattered with white.

SPRING WEDDING

overnight
once skeletal trees
decked in the finery
of a trillion pale green leaves
array themselves
against a sky as blue
as a baby's eyes

while brides and bridesmaids
sway in the morning breeze
plump ring bearers
and flower girls toss and
strew their petals

those more sober guests
who cannot bloom
line up along the path
wait for the nuptials
to begin

WALKING ON THE ESTUARY PATH

the tide is out, way out
beyond tall summer grasses gone to seed
black unseemly mud spreads far
a reminder that creation has an underside

at the tide line
a clump of fir stumps squat
like ship-wrecked sailors
their naked salt encrusted roots
rinsed twice each day
and bibbed afresh with seaweed

I turn away...
far down the path
my grandsons, miniature space men
in shining helmets
race back and forth
their bikes spin silver
flash metallic blue and green
one bike still sports training wheels

their parents in black spandex
hover, guardian angels
with no sign of sprouting wings
beneath their faded T- shirts
love sweats from their pores
engages their hands
moves the muscles of their arms
the air is charged with expectation
for these millennial children
flying into a future I will not see

Elizabeth Bartel

SWIMMING

In the warm water of the pool
I sink into another world
weightless
slowly breathing out.
Bubbles of air rise
where I lurk in the blue
like a deep-sea diver
behind my tinted goggles.

I flutter and kick
above a geometry of squares
between two black lines
past perfect circles of light
like ancient Cyclops
which stare unblinking
along the white tiled wall.

I turn my mouth to reach for air
as I must have reached for my mother's breast.
Breathe in and
for an instant water burbles soft
against my pillowed cheek.

Then face down into the depths
I breathe out again
crawling through that other world
to dim remembrance
of another age
spent in a primeval sea.

BETTER NOT TO THINK

Better not to think
of last time
when warmth of illicit wine
coursed through our veins.
With eyes half-closed
we watched marbled sirloin
spitting and hissing over glowing coals.
Smoke rose like a prayer
fragrant with thyme.
Virgin oil, balsamic vinegar
soaking into crusty bread.

Better not to think
of blue hyacinth, sweet and waxy,
standing tall in a shallow bowl
of polished stones,
silent witness in wavering candlelight
as our bodies move to the beat of jazz.
Your knowing hands, fingers
blurring the black and white
of piano keys.

You watching me. Me watching you.

And later, naked
among the twisted sheets,
our laughter
my unexpected tears
our melding skin
to sweating skin.

Better not to think of us
burning hot and quick
death unthought of
denying the taste of ashes
on the tongue.

GRIEF

His grief is hidden
like the rocky outcrop in a field
which takes centuries of rain and snow
to smooth down to this narrow seam,
only noticed by a ploughman,
a reaper, a harvester.

This man whom I can wound
so easily with just a look
or thoughtless word.
There is a secret tragedy
he takes upon himself
bears all alone,
another love, a heart
he holds close to his own
guards with his life.

Time goes by and all unknowing
a barrier has grown
around his heart, planted deep,
its concrete posts are strung
with smooth steel slats.
Not barbed wire. Never that.
He's a gentle man, ever fearful
of scarring me.

My darling love...
with a part of him sealed off.
Impregnable.

I WOULD RATHER HORSES

in the park a cavalcade
of motorcycles
wheel up the hill toward me
modern-day crusaders
eyes unseen behind protective glass
vests taped with red crosses
they sit low
their booted legs splayed
arms gloved in leather held wide,
they wheel abreast of me
in a thunderous roar
enveloped in smoke
and stench of burning oil

I would rather horses
towered over me
their harness brasses catching the light
rather a hundred hoofs
sidestepping briskly on the pavement
horses in good spirits
showing off
close enough for me to smell

SLIPPERS

Sky-blue quilted slippers, "foam treads"
from the thrift store,
almost new and just my size.

She did not wear them long, this E.E. Hammond.
Her initials marked in black ink
by a daughter, a niece?

I wonder how it was for E.E. Hammond
as she rose from her nursing bed,
smoothing down wisps of thin hair.

How she would have groped
with a prehensile toe
for the pretty blue things,
two playful bunnies at her feet,
then donned a bathrobe in matching blue.
She will have been a little vain,
fashion conscious.

Did she venture down
the long polished corridor, hold tight
to the smooth wooden railing along the walls?

Befuddled by drugs,
did she imagine herself
a Trans-Atlantic passenger
in a stormy sea on the decks of the Queen Mary?

I hope so. This E.E. Hammond...
in whose footsteps I so
blithely tread.

LISA AT THE POOL

I see Lisa at the pool.
Her fine dark hair curls gracefully
around a skull
which must have suffered
grievous passage
down a narrow birth canal.

I turn away. I cannot bear to look
at that sweet curve of waist and breast
clad neatly in black Lycra.
Lisa, brain damaged beauty queen,
eyes fringed by shadow.
My body's easy bend and stretch
insults the gross distortions of her limbs.

In the pool I see Lisa smile,
held in a kind embrace
her body swished to and fro
as one would a child
in the shallow waters of a lake.

I think of Lisa late at night.
Eighteen now. In her foster bed
menstrual blood must smear the sheet.
She could be raped,
conceive and bear a child,
not able to say a word,
the only sound a frenzied groan
or soft hum.

All the while, my body free.
I live my life.
And Lisa's heart beats on.

AFTER THE RAIN

Along this suburban lane
random puddles from an early shower
reflect blue sky, white clouds.
Kitchen windows stare into the sun.
An empty clothesline rattles
as squawking crows flare up
black flames, then settle
beside the spilling garbage cans.
Behind a chain-link fence
a child's brightly coloured swing
is padlocked waiting for school to end,
while unseen, a dog snuffles and yaps.

Further down the lane
beneath a canopy of darkest pine,
I tread on many years of fallen needles
springy as a mattress,
to come at last into a sunlit space
and see the old man's garden.

I think of blue-veined calloused hands
propping up the crooked branches
of an ancient apple tree,
while moss creeps over tilted paving stones.
Papery stalks of last year's hydrangeas
stand stiff and tall
beside his rotting canvas chair.
Rogue blackberries
have overtaken the broken shingles
and purple crocus crowd the snow-drops
fighting through last summer's grass.

"*Wait...wait* "
I want to shout,
"*Come back, come back old man!*
Look here...
your magnolia is about to bloom."

LAMENT

Lost love, I dreamt of you last night.
We were together at a feast you had prepared,
the table set, smoke rising from a barbecue.

At ease we talked of mundane things.
"*You died too soon*," I murmured,
"*I would have come.*"

"*Too bad*," you said and shrugged.
Your sleepy snake-eyes glinted.
"*We just missed each other. Ah well*," you sighed.

It seemed enough, then,
to feel the merest ache of sweetness in my loins,
touch the angry scar across your cheek,
forget the fated bottle arcing through the air,
harsh metal grinding, crashing...
the smell of burning rubber,
oil dripping slowly on the pavement.

I woke and remembered Jesus,
how he gathered up the derelicts,
wined and dined the drunks.

GRATITUDE

If we did not taste gratitude,
hidden in the warm sweetness
under the fuzzy softness
of a peach ripened by sun...

If we did not hear gratitude,
nor listen for
the ecstatic trills and ripples
pouring pure bliss
from the pulsing throat of a meadow lark...

If we did not feel gratitude,
would our hearts lurch
with a sudden knowing
of the unspeakable, invisible power
which slowly, slowly
unfolds the petals of a rose...

Then would salt tears sting,
run down our cheeks...

If we could not name gratitude?

ONE HAND CLAPPING

At the political meeting the room is crowded.
A bagpipe wails.
We rise to clap our famous Maude
down the centre aisle to the dais.

Two rows ahead a tall thin man waves
his right hand exuberantly.
Does he know her personally or is he waving
to a friend? *"Here, come here.*
There is an empty seat right here beside me."

Later when we are seated and
Maude is well into her talk,
people here and there in the crowd
applaud spontaneously.
I see the tall thin man
begin to wave again,
his left hand shriveled
like a broken twig.

With his right hand he keeps waving
waving, waving, his enthusiastic response.
I think of the essence good people leave behind
hanging in the air like precious perfume
long after they are gone.

Elizabeth Bartel

Vera Jensen is a mother, grandmother, great-grandmother, retired teacher, writer and gardener. The joys and fears, tears and laughter that these professions encompass are reflected in her poetry and prose. Vera was born in the Okanagan region of B.C. but lived for many years on the very edge of the ocean on the east coast of Vancouver Island, only recently moving a short way inland to the town of Comox.

Vera has had children's stories published in *Ranger Rick Magazine*, and in *Prentice Hall Ginn's Collections* series. Her poetry and prose have appeared in several magazines including *The Writer's Digest* and *A Room of One's Own*. She has also published articles and stories in a number of regional publications and local newspapers. Vera is also one of the co-founder's of the "Mostly Poets".

If you add in the general wear and tear, aches and pains of approaching old age, plus a generous dollop of imagination, with a good measure of faith, hope and love of her family, you will have Vera as she sees herself today.

TABLE OF CONTENTS

Circle Dance	39
Riches	40
On Summer Days	41
Black Socks	42
Moon Shadows	44
Hand In Hand	44
Hope	45
Moonstalker	45
Who Is That Old Woman	46
Fish Boat	47
Moon Song	48
Steps	49
Ordinary Women	50
Grandmothers	51
Water	52

CIRCLE DANCE

Chubby legs stomp on little square feet,
pink cheeks crease into a dimpled smile.
She dances.

Long arms, long legs, long braids
swing to the beat with coltish grace.
She dances.

Bright eyed, laughing,
inviting life and love with flying feet.
She dances.

A stronger rhythm draws her feet aside,
he leads her heart to heart.
They dance.

Children kick their feet up high,
she leads their joyous fling.
They dance.

Alone with memories and unforgotten dreams,
creaky knees, gnarled hands and aching feet
she hears the music call.
She dances.

RICHES

One morning a child with dimpled hands...
    wove coronets of dandelions.
    She wore the sun kissed bands
    till suppertime.

One day a girl stepped into womanhood...
    Solemn vows and golden rings
    created one where two had stood.
    Tiptoe with delight, they kissed.

One night a weary mother prayed...
    for all her sleeping treasure.
    Their golden heads were laid
    upon her heart.

Today a woman with gnarled hands...
    weaves coronets of dandelions
    lifts sun kissed bands
    to crown a laughing child.

ON SUMMER DAYS

It's early yet
the sun still gentle.
Crisp brown grass tickles my knees.
I crawl about the garden
collecting slugs.

Big green watering cans stand ready.
I dole out precious water
to veggies, roses and some favoured shrubs.
Snapdragons and calendula
survive in well-mulched beds.

The sun climbs higher.
I take my coffee to the deck.
Later...like the cat
I seek cool dappled shade
beneath the Maple tree,
wait for you to come to tea.

BLACK SOCKS

My grandson came to stay.
We hugged and hugged again
before he dumped his backpack in the guest room.
I reminded him, as grandmas do...

*"Dirty socks go in the hamper please
and underwear and shirts and jeans."*
"Yes, Gran," he said.

He never took the last three off
except perhaps to shower or swim.
But socks, black socks, dirty black socks...

*"Those black socks on the couch,
please put them in the hamper."*
"Yes, Gran," he said.
*"Those black socks hanging on the door,
please put them in the hamper."*
"Yes, Gran," he said.

Black socks, dirty black socks,
under chairs and tables
in the dog's basket...

"Put them in the hamper,"
I said each day.
"Yes, Gran," he said, and always did.
Black socks on the porch railings,
abandoned on the lawn.

"In the hamper,"
I pointed with my stick.
"Yes, Gran," he said.

All too soon he left again.
I went to tidy up that room,
and found...

One black sock beneath the pillow
and one beneath the mattress.
Three under the bed,
one in the bookcase.
Another one turned up
inside my rubber boot.

I washed and sorted,
then packed them off,
he phoned me in a week or so.

"*Thanks, Gran,*" he said,
"*I've changed,*" he said,
"*I'm wearing white ones now.*"

MOON SHADOWS

Whenever frozen moonlight glows
across the frosty lawn and shows
me shadows of another world than this
I remember how we used to kiss
before you spoke those words
that froze my heart.

HAND IN HAND

Eager for adventure
we stepped out on life's path together
undaunted by the twisting turns ahead.

When wearied by gaunt hills of worry
fear and toil
I would have fallen
you held me fast
showed me a straighter road.

When you faltered
heart broken
overcome with grief and pain
I held your hand.
My turn to lead the way.

We climb a little higher
still hand in hand
content to find a path
where we can walk together.

HOPE

Alone beneath grey skies
beside grey seas
on a still grey shore.

The rising sun tints mountain mists.
Between the darkest layers, rose deepens into gold.
Fiery rays of light creep out to touch the sea
retreat...
There'll be no sun today.

Tomorrow
or some tomorrow after that
dawn will paint away the grey.
Sunlight will dance upon the waves again.
Mourning will fade to memory.

MOONSTALKER

She stalks the moon
whenever stars are bright,
listens for a laugh
that once could vanquish night,
sees his shadow
traced on silvered lawn,
still hears his step.
She trails through moonlit rooms, bereft,
her restless feet impatient
for the dawn.
But he is gone,
and she must walk alone.

WHO IS THAT OLD WOMAN?

There is an old woman I often pass.
Through automatic doors of glass,
I see her standing awkwardly
smiling at me doubtfully.
Who she is, I do not know.
Perhaps we met once, long ago.

I see her in the window there.
We, both of us, have stopped to stare.
We lean upon our shopping carts
contemplating butter tarts.

She's rather stout, what can I say?
She limps a bit along the way.
Her hair is thin, her chins are double.
You think it's me? Then I'm in trouble.

I only see her at the mall.
In my mirror, not at all.
Never meet her while I'm weeding
raking, digging, hoeing, seeding.

Never see her at the beach
laughing children within reach.
Never see her when I'm dancing
(caught a glimpse once while romancing).

When I look beyond your shoulder
I can see that she is older...
No, my dear,
she can't be me.

Come and have a cup of tea.

FISH BOAT

Morning sun spotlights the scalloped wake
as a fish boat
slips across the somnolent sea.
The sand rustles.

Hist
      hist
           hist

chug of engines deepens the silence.

Slap
      slap
          slap

The fish boat's wake strikes a brief counterpoint
to the ancient rhythm of the sea.
Watchers see stabilizers and antenna rise
like feelers on some prehistoric predator.

Seabird
      cries
          questions

man's ancient need for Exploitation.

MOON SONG

The restless ocean whispers secrets to the sand
as lovers
hand in hand
pause to catch their breath
and stand
as they have often done throughout the years
beneath the moon.
They've shared their laughter, hopes and tears
they've shared success and daunting fears.
Yet they must face the parting death commands
release the other's gnarled familiar hands.
But now,
they kiss as lovers do
whisper
I love you
beneath the moon.
They cling for just one moment more
aware that each must pass alone
through that great door.
But for tonight, they walk on
hand in hand
content to be together on the sand
beneath the moon.

STEPS

He struggled from the womb
to yell defiance at the too bright world
until warm arms and breast
could satisfy his needs.

She kept him close until he stood alone
hands reaching for some treasure or a surer hold
he shrugged away her grasp.

Her hands were there to catch him if he fell
he took a step,
and then another step away
she let him go.

He ran to find what lay beyond the door
she scooped him up,
he has a lifetime yet
to find that outer world.

ORDINARY WOMEN

They meet for lunch,
just ordinary women.
Yet each creased and crumpled face
tells a story.

A wartime job in some top-secret ministry
years of service in the military
husbands, brothers, lost.
Lives torn apart, uprooted, changed.
Ordinary...?

They survived, raised families.
One cooked for twenty men at harvest time
until they sold the farm.
One had her youngest child on board a fishing boat.
Another found herself in Chile, Spain and Africa
each new home a challenge and another baby.

They share their stories,
joke about hardships, brag about good times.
Look back with wonder at their younger selves.
"*It seems like yesterday,*" they say.

Lines trace the tears they've shed
the worry, the laughter,
the love they've shared.
Hands worn with care and pain
still knit and crochet, bake.

The "wrinklies" they call themselves
cheerful volunteers in soup kitchens,
thrift shops, hospices,
nurturing grandchildren.

Ordinary women
taking time for lunch...
together.

GRANDMOTHERS

Cereal, skim milk a little fruit
I sigh over my skimpy breakfast
I'm dieting again...

> Today
> my dark skinned sister
> shared meager bowls of rice and beans
> with orphaned grandchildren.

My salad bowl is heaped with greens
tomatoes, peppers, and a little cheese
I smile as I count calories and carbs...

> My sister hears
> children crying with hunger
> before dawn
> she'll dig some roots to share.

On Sunday...
I add an envelope marked, missions
to my weekly offering...

> Daily
> my sister offers thanks
> for life, laughter,
> and these children she still has.

WATER

Water in abundance.
Celebrate our wealth.

Morning
Revel in your morning shower.
Brush your teeth.
Taste the water
as you swallow
vitamins and pills.
Savour every drop of morning brew.

Imagine fetching water from a common well.

Noon
Listen to the burble of the coffee urn at work.
Admire the beauty of the water cooler.
Fill your cup
then tip the last drops down the drain.
You only needed just a sip or two
to quench your thirst.

Imagine walking miles to reach a muddy water hole.

At work
My workspace boasts a desk and chair.
A water bottle rests beside
the cooling coffee cup.
I share my lunch with you
crisp salad greens
iced tea with sprig of mint.

Imagine working in the heat waiting for the water carrier's
cart.

Afternoon
Wash your hands,
germs linger everywhere.
Our staff room's clean and bright
facilities are scrubbed
our privacy protected.
The air conditioner sucks excess moisture
from the air we breathe.

Imagine waiting till it's dark to find a vacant lot.

Evening
Listen to the swish and swirl
as washers scrub and rinse and rinse again.
Turn on the hose to wash the car
swirl suds about and wipe the dirt away
or scatter water liberally
on lush green lawns.

Imagine rusty water dribbling from the village tap.

Vera Jensen

For Tress,

lovingly,

Marieluisa

♡

May 2015

Marieluisa Auterson was born in Switzerland, but moved to Canada in 1980, where she married her second husband. She is a wife, mother and grandmother of six grandchildren.

Marieluisa is a Swiss/American Psychologist and an internationally known researcher and lecturer in the field of body/mind integration. Her poetry centers around human frailty, healing and the path to God. Many of her poems were written to help clients move on in their life.

In her poetry, Marieluisa tries to initiate a cathartic feeling, a mood swing. She likes to stir up deep emotions and move them towards a playful, peaceful outlook in life.

Marieluisa is a charter member of the "Mostly Poets". *"A poem is never finished,"* she says. *"It is an interlude, a pause like breath held between inhaling and exhaling."* She is currently working on her book *Kindle the Flame of Love.*

TABLE OF CONTENTS

"PATHS IN BETWEEN"

Beginnings:
God Is   57
Dawn   58

Opening:
Conception   59
Plenty   60
Dance   60

Searching:
Good Life Blues   61

Sharing:
The Rope   62
Raised   63

Love:
Distance   64

Loss:
Miscarriage   65
The Passing   66
Rest Oh My Soul   67

Celebrating:
Celebration   68
Beyond Ashes   69
Birth   70
The Poem   71

GOD IS

GOD
    IS...
        the light
        the sound
        the message

        I fear and tremble
        in surrender
        as I open to His
    ALL...
        cradle
        of space-less
        abundance

Marieluisa Auterson

DAWN

I searched
for light in my soul many a time
there seemed to be none

just desert bleakness

grey shadow-less vastness

empty mummified moments

I waited long
for visions of dawn
behind the dark hills

where light so ancient
strikes the heart's closure
warmth floods the limbs
eyes open to see

the shine of daybreak

CONCEPTION

It feels
as if...

a thought...
conceived while stroking clouds with open hands
like children play
is floating down
to touch the barren ground on which I stand
with naked feet

earth...
releases tiny sparks of warmth
that move my guts
thrill my heart

fire...
shared with earth's molten essence
stirs my belly
drives the thought to grab my mind

form...
arises shaped by sight and
shakes my being with its presence

> *I am*
> a mold where the invisible
> is molded out of night

> *I am*
> a spark of joy when
> kissed by light

PLENTY

God promised
"There will be plenty"

What if I perish...
in pitch black darkness
chained to past thoughts, past deeds
staring at my starvation
reflected back from all angles
in the hollowed caves of my shortcomings
cluttered with debris

or is it compost
decomposing...
turning to fertile ground
holding the flowers of my soul
in new visions of light

God whispers
*"There is plenty...
call me, trust me"*

DANCE

moments
of dance with you

steps of intimacy
tightly nestled

two as one
rocking life moves
in breezy space

lovers...
in time suspended

GOOD LIFE BLUES

How can I write a poem
when life rolls along
endless assembly lines of
days, nights
joys, pains
highs and lows?

When what I feel
is nothing but
a food-filled stomach
and feet, warm, cozy
stretched out
toward a roaring fire?

Affluent society's numbing
has caught up with me.

Yet, there is a terror in my heart
that screams... *"Is this it?*
Where are all the wild dreams?"

Gone, drowned, drowned out by
wealth, security, safety, age.

> I step out on the balcony
> beckoning, calling.
> Moonlight filters through the trees.
> It's cold...I shiver.
> Breathing deep
> I fill my lungs with damp night air,
> they become balloons ready to float away.
> With a long moanful *"aaah..."*
> I let go.
>
> *"Here I am,"*
> I say, after a while.
> *"This is it."*

Marieluisa Auterson

THE ROPE

I thought
you were a rope
to hold onto

I thought
you were securely fastened
to the rocks
we jointly climbed

I found
instead that you
lost your footing
expected me to be a rope for you

holding hands
we tumbled
down the mountain

when the ground
gave way
under our feet

> *"Oh Lord!*
> *Let me hold only onto Thee"*
> but...

you were wrapped in darkness

RAISED

Cancer
this time the kidneys
a man still in his youth
lovely face

He shares his story
tells of despair
tormenting desires
petrified scared
unwept bitter sadness...

> *Together we move*
> *beyond space, beyond time*
> *where life meets death's calling*
> *where fear grabs hold of the Divine*
>
> *Horror, gasping*
> *tears streaming, pain*
> *heart stretches, heart opens*
>
> *Visions of mountains, flowers, music*
> *gently lift*
> *resistance to passing*
>
> *Eyes suddenly radiant*
> *cheeks hollowed, glowing*
> *body lightens...*

Breathless...
arms outstretched
he holds onto invisible hands

hands that reached down to raise him

Marieluisa Auterson

DISTANCE

When I am distant from your heart
    I tread darkly
    with silent steps on fallen leaves
    fog clouds my soul
    it is winter

When I am distant from your heart
    I plug my ears with cotton wool
    while voiceless echoes
    hammer doors with bloody fists
    keys are lost

I crouch on steps outside the gate
    search for cracks where light spills through
    catch a glimpse of how you live
    to reassure my heart

When I am distant from your heart
    I long for times when bathed in sun
    we danced to tunes unheard by ears
    and swam in blueness
    melting in each other's eyes

I plead with God to crumble walls
    like St. Peter's cell
    I stretch my heart until it breaks
    grasp the innocence from which we hide

When I am distant from your heart
    time's move is slow

MISCARRIAGE

The surgeon's clever hands
scraped out what was left
of the tiny baby in her womb
flesh spent
soul returned to God.

I see her
tall, slim
walking with a straight back.
She has been out running
looks a bit sweaty.

Sweat,
or is it burning tears
dry on hot cheeks,
barely wetting the desert
of her empty heart.

Her voice sounds deep, yet somewhat flat
crushed by the weight of pain.

"King David mourned seven days
for his dying son," she says.
"When the child was dead,
he washed himself, worshipped God
ate some food, went on
with his daily business."

Her eyes search the horizon.
She smiles.

"We can try again," she says.
"I will shower now."

"Oh, Soul mate,
how I love your bravery."

THE PASSING

So sudden!
the news...
killed abroad

> I sit
> slouched
> a moment ago
> heart full of joy
> body full of vigor

> Now tearless
> eyes burning
> head moving like a pendulum
> left right, left right
> *No! No!*

> Endless moments
> I try to breathe
> thoughts following the beloved
> into the dark land,
> > hold him
> > hold him
> > hold him...

I question,
"Is he really in the light,
where is my knowing?"
Head still shaking
Left right, left right

Timeless flow...

Pained heart
beyond grief
open
still
sharing undying love

REST, OH MY SOUL

Threads in the wind, blown in all directions
spider's broken web
the wind is fierce
the spider left

Shells on the beach, strewn over pebbles
oysters' broken homes
the sea is fierce
the oysters gone

Oh my Soul!
I tumble through life's thrashings
my heart is numb
my stars are distant

Be still
Take time for resting

CELEBRATION

Shivers
run up and down my spine
burst onto the skin
waken my heart

Joy
rushes through spider web vessels
mingles with vision of light
turns golden
reflects in vast ocean of mind

Sound
resonates in my ears
curling, swirling
threads of silver
floating in midair

Jubilee
captures echoes of melodies
louder...louder
lighter...lighter

and merges
in subtlest softness with

song ever being

BEYOND ASHES

"let's dance once more"
he says and
plays old tunes
sweet
lulling
dead
long buried in the maze of memory

"no"
I say
I will not waltz on scattered ashes
stirring bones
skeletons of hope
dust
floating in midair

give me
new ground
a polished ballroom
with cool clean marble floor
where we can swing together
once again
weightless

yet

I find myself alone
stamping an ancient rhythm
on old trampled earth
a gentle breeze
upholds my swirling body
caresses my outstretched arms
my naked feet
rustle in the leaves

I have forgiven

BIRTH

All changed
clouds removed
brilliance
transcending heart's seas
in depths unstirred

The new
born again
in petal dew purity
with petal soft fingers
touched and held

Arms open to nurture
breasts open to feed
radiance
filling heart's vastness
in love unhinged

Oh...joy
Oh...fullness of body
Oh...fullness of heart

THE POEM

As I trip
over old urges, dreams
I lie weak, broken, chained.
No hero in sight to rescue me
even God seems absent.

A little thought speaks to me,
"Interesting experience," it says.
"I wonder how you will glue yourself back together?"

"I'll pray," I say,
"I'll write a poem.."

Here it is.

Marieluisa Auterson

Sharon Tilton Urdahl, is a poet, writer, multimedia artist and before retirement, a successful businesswoman who owned and operated an art gallery for over fifteen years. A "free spirit," Sharon was encouraged in her youth to pursue her passion for the arts. She was born in Pioneer Mines, B.C. and finds herself often *"reflecting back to that quiet place of beginnings."* Vancouver was home for most of her life, but for the past twenty-eight years she has lived in rural Comox, on Vancouver Island with her husband Hans...*"who I especially thank for his ongoing support and encouragement."*

Sharon writes of her love and spiritual connection to nature, family and the world around her. She creates poetic vignettes of personal history and the human experience of others. She says, "M*y poetry often introduces people who either helped shape me, or have shared my path...I hope when reading my poetry, others, especially my children and grandchildren will gain a understanding of who and why I am...finding words or thoughts that somehow reach them at a deeper level."*

 She has had numerous articles published in magazines and newspapers and is a founding member of a "Circle of Writers" and longstanding member of the "Mostly Poets" critique group.

TABLE OF CONTENTS

The Nest   75

Wash Day   76

Sweet Seventeen   77

Our Mother's Bones   78

Until I Taste The Salt   79

First Time Radiation   80

This Day   81

Sandra's Prayer Flags   82

The Hummingbird   83

Posmuki   84

The Blood Remembers   85

Brenda's Wish   86

Full Moon Swimming   87

Moon Baptismal   88

Memories Of Seoul – Olympic Park   89

THE NEST

In early morn
when my sleeping house is still
and waking souls
are caught in dawn's fine net,
I take my tea to the garden.

First bird welcomes
the rising sun
and a choir of warblers
fills the silence.
Red breast swollen with life
a robin gathers twigs
comes back for tufts
of dewy moss and
last year's broken ties
from a newly budding rose.

As light slips
through the forest canopy,
I release my hair
from its tightly wound coil,
brush night from silver strands,
gather forgotten dreams
caught in tangles, then roll them
into a soft, small ball.

Opening my hand
I show my offering.
The tiny bundle of fine grey hair
lifts from my open palm
carried upward on the wind
silently as a mother's prayer.
With one grateful swoop
the robin catches the airborne gift then
hastens to weave my silken threads
into her own downy nest.

Sharon Tilton Urdahl

WASH DAY

Saturday afternoon,
mom would bring the wash
in from the line...

With red chapped hands
she draped stiff,
frozen clothes
over backs of wooden chairs.

The small kitchen filled
with scent of pine,
fresh new snow.

Winter's breath,
still trapped in ice clad threads of
snow-bleached sheets, sparkled
then quickly dried, in the warmth
from her sawdust fueled stove.

Droplets of melting snow,
formed tiny pools
on a worn linoleum floor.

Came night...
and I, snuggly tucked in
crisp, clean sheets and
cozy flannel pajamas,
thought only of angels
I had made in softly
falling snow.

SWEET SEVENTEEN

You and I,
sweet seventeen...
smile at the camera.

In the photo...
You wear a straight blue skirt,
matching cashmere *"twin sweater"* set,
a shy look of innocence, naivety...
I was *"cool,"*
wearing pink and grey saddle shoes,
hot pink skirt ballooning
over two starched crinolines,
face framed by a white *"Peter Pan"* collar.
My eyes challenge the lens...

You and I,
so young,
caught by the camera...

Standing on the steps of King Ed High,
flanked by crouching grey stone lions,
guardians of the doors to our last year
of *"wordy wisdom"*...
Taken early spring, only
days before we graduated.
Schoolbooks pressed to our breasts,
the two of us so eager to embrace a world
where all unplanned lessons waited.

Two springs later...
You...married.
I...a mom.

You and I,
both still young...
both still learning.

OUR MOTHER'S BONES

The three of us,
newly orphaned,
scrunch together on the
front seat of Bob's truck.

Our grief, despair and tears
contained in a small
white cardboard box,
are carried on Diana's lap...
my sister's hand rests on the lid.

Our destination being neither
here nor there
but somewhere
in between...

We want no heavy,
earth blanket for her eternity,
life was enough.
We find a place
where calm water
gently nudges shore...
Our mother's bones lie there.

Her silky casket,
light, transparent
has no restricting walls.
Released from earthy weight,
she moves easily with the ocean's
ebb and flow...

Resting now,
she is witness to seasons of the land,
greets the rising sun, passing moon
and distant stars.
In death...
she is.

UNTIL I TASTE THE SALT

Fading light
edges the shore
with gold and pink.
Gulls on the water
form a lifeline,
then with raucus cry
follow the leader
up and away.

Crow dips his beak
in reflecting pools,
tilts back his head
to swallow the sun's last rays.
Like a traveling salesman
with black suit shining,
he leaves on a solo flight north.

Pipers race,
dodge waves,
leave their marks
along the sandy beach.
A lone loon wails
into the darkening night.
I am not aware I am answering
until I taste the salt.

FIRST TIME RADIATION 1996
Meditation

Afraid of the unknown
I try to quiet my mind,
find empty space,
I tell my self...

> *relax*
> *breathe easy*
> *breathe deep*
> *breathe out*
> *slowly*
> *slowly*
> *breathe*

Suddenly,
silent hoofs charge the sky.
Spirited away, I am above it all,
powder puff clouds stand still
as deer and I race
past time.
Tightened muscles relax,
peace and calm surround us,
distance me from reality...
radiation.

This moment...
we are one,
deer and I.
Alone in the vastness of my journey
I cling to her...
feel her warmth,
smell her wildness,
my hair a cape of silk
flags the sky.
Lost in the darkness...
brilliant stars light a path
to worlds unknown as
silence and peace surround us...

Endless galaxies stretch
like hopeful guides before me.
Suspended in time
we move effortlessly,
glide fearlessly through the dark.
This is my peace, my place
this deep, deep,
sacred universe...
where time stands still.

Lying on my back
I hear the radiation machine... *Stop*

THIS DAY

Dropped by the passing sun,
wavering threads of pink and mauve
slip beyond the horizon.
Shallow pools, residue from the last tide
reflect the stillness of a cloudless sky.

Small beach craters become havens for
tiny crabs, lost feathers, a purple starfish.
All patiently wait for the moon and
their eternal dance
with the sea.

Memories...
pressed in fading footprints,
are slowly erased
at water's edge
taking this day
with them.

SANDRA'S PRAYER FLAGS

When I awoke
first thoughts were of you.
I felt a tug in my heart,
anxious...
I knew this would be the day.
It is the way with you and me,
our lives unfolding
on parallel paths,
blood link seemingly
more sister than cousin.
Distance... never a barrier
we feel
the other.

This evening,
I watch Tibetan prayer flags,
hung after your cancer diagnosis,
flutter bravely between my apple trees.
Once bright red, white,
blue, yellow, and green
they are now battle worn.
Faded from wind and rain
tattered...threadbare.

Like startled birds
released from a cage,
they suddenly rise in the breeze
wave wildly...
Their printed galloping black horses,
laden with prayers
in a language I do not know,
carry my fears with them.
I feel
your goodbye.

Eulogy for Sandra Jorgensen

THE HUMMINGBIRD

I turn soil,
ready my garden for new life,
remember you while I work...
plant tiny blue Forget-me-nots
transparent California poppies.

A hummingbird visits the feeder
outside the kitchen window.
I remember you smiling,
hear you say...

*"I will come back you know,
but only as a hummingbird. "*

I imagine you here, now,
as that tiny bird...
sporting flashy ruby throat
instead of beautiful red hair.

You...
visiting my garden,
tasting California poppies,
forget-me-not.

POSMUKI

Kneeling on the little white chair,
she is hunched over the play table.
A growing quilt of discarded,
bright coloured paper
spreading on the floor.
Crayon drawings embellish each piece.

Red, orange, blue and green,
hearts, rainbows, figures
with smiling faces,
long flowing hair,
purple butterflies and
bright yellow sunshine
fill empty spaces.

Tiny fingers curl around a purple crayon.
Her serious face hovering close
to the surface of the paper.
Tongue tip moving
back and forth across her lips,
she concentrates on each letter
carefully printed on the paper.

Awkwardly scribed, a message inches
across the bottom of the page.
I watch as she prints out each letter.
P   O   S   M   U   K   I
finally a long sigh...
holding the picture in front of herself,
Jasmin shows her finished masterpiece...

A large multi-coloured heart
fills the center,
drawn close to it,
a tiny red and yellow butterfly...

"*You and me,*" she says...
a smile stretching across her face.
After much praise,
I inquire about the bold letters
marching across the bottom...
"N*ana,*" she says in a voice
gently tinted with disbelief,
and surprise that I need ask...

"*Posmuki means I love you.*"

THE BLOOD REMEMBERS

Carrying a tiny blue bundle,
my son gently places his newborn
into my waiting arms.
Baby scent fills me.
Warmth of the moment
unlocks sleeping memories...
I rock my grandson instinctively
to ancient rhythms
heard in the depth
of my mothering soul.
Soft dark grey, squinting eyes
peer deep into mine.
I know he sees me...
I swim those calming pools
while unheard whispers
of recognition flow between us.
The blood remembered...
traced the map, chose
a perfect pattern, then
showed me a path to
eternal life...

85

BRENDA'S WISH

We are not really close friends,
still, you have called late
this cold, February night,
asked me to take you to the lantern festival.

You have a cough, low-grade fever...
I worry about taking you out,
you insist you are fine
will dress warmly...
How can I deny you?

As I drive, you share your life...
tell me your stepfather served in the British Army,
that you grew up in Malaysia,
had seen lanterns released as a child,
wanted to see them again tonight,
one more time.

Four paper lanterns are to be sent skyward.
Oblivious to the gathering crowd,
you study each fragile beacon
as it is raised for it's flight
into the clear night sky,
fueled only by the candle it holds inside.

Your eyes never leave the flickering flame.
Holding your breath...
you watch intently as they wobble upward,
then slowly exhale...
as though helping each lantern lift.

Knowing prayers travel with them,
I send my own...

The lanterns drift upward,
we watch until each one disappears,
melting into the twinkling heavens...
until they can no longer be distinguished
from a distant shooting star
falling on the horizon...

Later, we celebrate the night:
are decadent, drink hot coffee,
eat chocolates,
laugh...

Eulogy for Brenda Slater
(Brenda passed away the following spring from breast cancer.)

FULL MOON SWIMMING

Bare limbs create a milky silhouette
against the darkening sky.
Loosened hair, a dark halo of bobbing curls.
Poised like a wingless angel
eager to soar,
she submerges
in the cool night water...

Drummers on shore witness
the crescent of full moon
slowly rising from the ocean floor.
Shimmering serpentine reflections
waver on the water surface,
casting the swimmer
a golden lifeline to shore.

MOON BAPTISMAL

Your silent return
wakes me
from deepest sleep.
Witness to your rising grace,
ancient memory
pulls me into rhythms
of nocturnal dance.

It is not just me
who feels urging whispers
released from the throat of night...

Dormant instincts stir as
owl stretches transparent wings,
silently glides from inky shadows.
Her watchful eyes unblinking as
creatures with soft padded paws
hide from flooding light.

You rise and glide
across the bejeweled sky.
My welcoming hands reach to
hold shimmering moonbeams.
Bathed in peace,
your cloak of light
surrounds me,
blesses me
wholly.

MEMORIES OF SEOUL - OLYMPIC PARK

I

Golden Gingko leaves,
chased by cool October winds
race across grey stepping-stones.
Like ancient I Ching coins tossed
by a wise fortune teller,
they predict the coming winter.

II

Dried from summer heat,
white flower heads
nod tiredly in cool autumn air.
A sudden breeze stirs the pond,
falling Gingko leaves and I
are caught in winter's current.

III

Bronze and gold leaves
released from ancient arms.
So many thoughts float free...
Gripped by scent of souring earth,
as year after year, each day
is pressed into aging soil.
With the coming of winter,
I know I am part of it all.

IV

A magpie watches
a falling Gingko leaf brush my lips,
carry unspoken words
across the quiet lake.
My thoughts are heard
only by bowed heads of silver grasses.
Magpie clicks his tongue,
converses with autumn's breeze.
Reminds me...
good-byes are difficult.

Sharon Tilton Urdahl

Katherine Kane, artist, writer, poet and teacher, is known for her outgoing personality and love of life and people. Widely traveled and exposed to different cultures, Katherine has drawn upon her rich life experiences as a source for her creativity.

Raised in Appalachia in south-eastern Ohio, Katherine grew up on a farm in an extended family. She later moved to Lexington, Kentucky, heart of the Bluegrass. In 2004, Katherine and her husband John, moved to the Pacific Northwest on Vancouver Island to experience living near the ocean and mountains.

Deeply intuitive, Katherine listens to nature, the symbolism of dreams, and to her inner voice. Katherine's artistic interpretation, be it written or visual, is a reflection of her keenly attuned sensitivity to the spirit of the universe and to the majesty of its eternal wisdom.

"I have always loved words. I love choosing them, playing with them, arranging them on the page...I like to make them dance. Working with words is much like developing photographs in the darkroom. You can take a blank piece of paper and watch the images appear...it is painting pictures with words."

91

TABLE OF CONTENTS

Hope Afloat	93
Condos Rising	94
West Coast Winters	95
In Silence	96
Tending The Graves	98
Separate Selves	99
Traveling To Somewhere	100
Language Barrier	101
Southern Summers	102
"As American As"	103
For Jan	103
Trust Jesus	104
No More Sadness	105
Dream Catcher	106
The Last Dance	107

HOPE AFLOAT

I hear the drumbeat
the rhythmic beat
from the lone drummer at the back of the dragon boat

the paddlers
survivors of breast cancer
moving their oars in unison to the drumming
through the grey-blue waters of the estuary

we are all survivors
of one thing or another

we all experience loss of some kind
whether it be the loss of a body part
the loss of a loved one
or the loss of a way of life

like the paddlers
we push forward
overcoming resistance

the drumbeat
our heartbeat
ringing out in hope

hope is afloat

CONDOS RISING

mountains in Prussian blue
backlit with a golden glow
from the setting sun
give form to the painting
in my mind's eye
at the horizon line
shades of Hooker's green
create rows of Douglas fir
set back like bleachers
in a stadium

at water's edge
washes of Ultramarine blue
brush lightly across
my Arches paper
shaping gentle waves
as the tide fills Courtenay Estuary

dots of Chinese white
fill billowing sails
of the occasional boat
sailing around Goose Spit
I sit in my artist's chair
at the studio window
lost in a painter's meditative state

noise of machinery
breaks my trance
the scene on my easel slowly replaced
as steel beams and concrete walls
rise above ground level
flat topped man-made mesas
beginnings of a desert scene
not natural to Vancouver Island

condos rising on Comox Avenue

WEST COAST WINTERS

greys come creeping
over mountains
spilling over peaks
oozing in and out of crevices
unfolding a soft flannel blanket
that covers the horizon line
connecting land to sea

greys come dancing
over the water
skipping over beach rocks
tiptoeing across the pier
hiding boats in the harbour
with fishermen
selling their day's catch

greys wander aimlessly
up the narrow streets
encircling people shapes
in the village

greys swirl through tall fir trees
narrow tendrils of smoky haze
illuminating their swaying branches
with an iridescent glow

greys come sneaking
peeping through windows
spying   prying
whispering
in mystical mysterious ways

IN SILENCE

My father doesn't have much to say
as he is often silent.
His silence is not due to absence
of thought, however.
His mind pulsates
with ideas on the universe
the plight of man
the wonder of what lies beyond.

His thoughts are slow
to emerge with voice.
It takes him a long time
to express ideas.
Those close to him
are impatient.
Even though, when they take the time
they are amazed at the depth
and wisdom of his words.

Most of the time, those he wishes
to speak with are too busy.
His wife is the least receptive.
She isn't good at listening
keeps interrupting
so he sits in silence.

He retreats to his room
reclines on his bed
the mattress lumpy from years of use.
He doesn't sleep much
but reads books that I bring him.
Books on Zen and mysticism and such.
I steer him away from cheap paperbacks
that he picks up in the grocery store.

My father and I discuss
his recent readings.
But because of his slow pace and
the time it takes to express his thoughts
I grow impatient.
I make excuses to leave
or my mother interrupts.

Sometimes my father sits at his typewriter
typing his thoughts on white index cards.
But the time it takes to transfer his thoughts
from his mind to the keyboard
prevents him from creating
much written material.
He is better arranging his thoughts in his head
so he becomes silent
lost in his ideas without interruption
without being rushed by others.

He sorts his ideas as he works in his garden
tosses them in his head as he turns the soil
working in the earth is conducive to thinking.
He can do it at his own speed
on his own terms.
My father speaks his words in silence.

TENDING THE GRAVES

I tend the graves
on birthdays and holidays
hemlock wreaths in December
peonies on Memorial Day
in honour of cousin Ray
killed in the Second World War

my mother's family name
is engraved on the large marker
serving as the headstone
for the five people buried beneath it
all sharing the same surname
except for my father
misfit in death as in life

I tend the graves
planting crocus and daffodil
clearing away fallen leaves
and other signs of winter decay
I prepare their resting places
for the coming spring

I go to the graves
on lonely days
to ease my pain of separation
longing to make contact
I search for signs of spirit

I stand at the graves
waiting
for the faintest feeling of family
but there is only the void

their spirits
must be soaring elsewhere
the wind blowing through rows of cedar
in the musty smells of fall
or the sunsets that cast an orange glow
their decaying bodies
no longer house their souls

SEPARATE SELVES

brother and sisters
created from the same mold
we grew up together
in the white country farmhouse
sharing birthdays
Christmases

childhoods passing
we developed separate selves
searching for our identity
so different
yet like that mold
from whence we began our journey

TRAVELING TO SOMEWHERE

Tonight...on a train from Rome...
I lean out the window
breathe in the rushing air
cooled by the speed of the train
gazing out onto the countryside
I catch silhouettes of trees and houses
my eyes set on the stars
and yellow pin-spots of villages on the horizon

I think of you...
the times we fantasized hopping trains
riding the tracks to unknown places
my fantasies are now realities
the tracks long and boring
staring at this unfamiliar land
I long for home
packed like cattle in a boxcar
along with others
headed somewhere

I share a berth with an elderly man and woman
the old man is ill
they close all the windows
I move to the aisle...escape the smothering heat
an express train rushes by
the impact throwing me against the wall
stunned...I reposition myself
my hair blows in the wind
briefly I find solitude...

a conductor walks by...shuts the window
as I reopen it, two Italian men eye me
not impressed with their style of flirting
I make signs of *"Good Night"*
awkwardly I climb to my top berth
the air stale
the ride rough
will I sleep tonight
will I awake for my destination

remember when we dreamed of hopping trains
and riding to I don't know where...

LANGUAGE BARRIER

jibber, jibber, jabber
one continuous clatter
all your foreign tongues
blending into one
deafening roar

it's not that I dislike you
I just desire others like me
while traveling unknown roads
hearing sounds I could decode
would be music to my ears

meanwhile I remain outnumbered
so I attempt to slumber
pretending that I'm home
with friends of my own
who speak my language

SOUTHERN SUMMERS

lazy summer evenings spent on verandas
legs dangle
bare toes push white wicker swings
back and forth

warm night sounds of cicadas
nighthawks and bats
descend in circling patterns
feast on mosquito dinners

slow swinging
lemon slices and fresh mint
float in tall glasses of iced tea
sporadic moments of coolness
as condensation drips

cats in repose
extensions of porch railings
brought only to life by movement
sounds of creatures
who roam the night

easy chatter
southern drawls roll off tongues
as neighbours on evening strolls
linger
comment on the weather

sweet scent of jasmine...gardenia
gently waft through moist air
a blanket of warm hospitality
covers southern shoulders

"AS AMERICAN AS"

six o'clock in the afternoon
New York City...hello
I see you gazing back at me
in all your gory splendour
mile on mile
of multi-coloured machines
the tight lipped smiles
of those running away
from their big apple

FOR JAN

unexpectedly...
that feeling of aloneness
isolation
of living a life that doesn't matter
is shattered
broken apart
by a moment of kindness
the spoken words of another
speaking of the unspeakable
acknowledging
accepting
both the visible and invisible me

a simple
but powerful act of showing
that my life matters

TRUST JESUS

"Trust Jesus"
read the words painted in red
on the wooden sign nailed to a palm tree
along the two-lane road toward the beach.

Trust Jesus?
Trust what to Jesus?
Your thoughts, your secrets, your money
your body, your soul?

Trust Jesus
like you trust your mother, your spouse
or trust that you will make it
through another day?

Take the sign
"Get Right with God."
Get what right with God?
What was wrong in the first place?

Or *"Jesus Saves."*
Jesus saves what?
Aluminum cans, plastic twist ties
or rubber bands like my mother saves?

Money perhaps?
Does he have a savings account
stocks and bonds
or real estate?

What if a sign read *"Trust Yourself?"*
Would you trust yourself
to do what you need to do
make the right decisions
live your life according
to your inner self?

Or is it easier to just trust Jesus?

NO MORE SADNESS

I will read the best seller on self-improvement
get involved in another psychological movement
I can finance therapy for only dollars a day
anything to make my life a little more gay
for I will have no more sadness in my life

I must start practicing yoga again
keeping my body supple and thin
mega-vitamins three times a day
helps me look younger and my hair less grey
and there will be no more sadness in my life

I can try out those new sexual techniques
that I read about only last week
which promise instant erotic pleasure
they say can be scientifically measured
oh I will have no more sadness in my life

I could get one more advanced degree
as improving the intellect makes a better me
and if I am always kind and good
living out my karma as I should
then there will be no more sadness in my life

DREAM CATCHER

last night in the darkness
my dream catcher drew you in
long ago memories tangled
in the threads and feathers
carefully crafted by wise hands

forty years had not aged you
you looked exactly as I remember
your hair combed back like Elvis
wide grin too large for your face
eyes that were never truthful

you were so confident
like nothing had ever changed
as if I would be thrilled to see you
resume where we once left off

with cheerful anticipation
you suggested we leave together

I replied, *"I am no longer twenty-one"*

THE LAST DANCE

soft afternoon rain
falls in Box Canyon
I crouch
clasp my arms around my knees
lean back on my haunches
watch the leaves say goodbye
to another year

death is saved for last
it is the greatest high
the leaves
tell me this is surely so

tulip poplars
elm...birch...oak
tower over me
rising just above the rim of sheer rock
that form the sides of the canyon
synchronizing their flight downwards
each leaf chooses its route
to the ground below

some go quickly
twirl...descend in spirals
rest on the canyon floor
others glide through the air
waltzing back and forth

one tulip poplar leaf
swoops and soars like an eagle
beginning another journey
to new heights
I lean forward as it drifts by me
I whisper...
*"thank you for saving
the last dance for me"*

Jan Bush spent many years as an English teacher. She has raised a family and now enjoys her grandchildren, writing and growing prize-winning dahlias in her garden by the sea.

A poet, writer and singer, Jan is an active member of "Scribblers" writers' group and was a co-founding member of "Mostly Poets". She is also founder of Comox Valley's, North Island Elder College, Writers' Workshop.

Jan has been published in several journals, magazines and newspapers and won several awards for her poetry. She writes of all aspects of life, spanning most ranges of emotion, but has a particular gift of being able to bring a touch of lightness and humour into much of her poetry.

She loves poetry with a passion, and has been a reader at many local events. Always wanting to encourage others who write, Jan hopes new poets, and especially young poets will be inspired and emerge from all the public readings.

TABLE OF CONTENTS

Hats   111

Hands   112

This Old Gate   113

Ashes   114

Tom Cat   115

Night Prowler   116

Child's Play   117

Christmas In Tyrol   118

Animal Eyes   120

At The Edge Of The Woods   121

Elk   122

Two Scenes   123

Oh Canada   124

Sisters   125

HATS

Oh how I hate hats
I know they're for your head
don't wear them in the bathtub
don't wear them in your bed.

But if the wind is blowing
to keep your ears so snuggly
you wear them in the winter
when the weather gets quite ugly.

And as for at a baseball game
my mom remarked it's wise
to wear a peaked baseball cap
keeping sun out of your eyes.

While riding on a frisky horse
put a helmet on your head
cause if that stallion bucks you off
you'll never end up dead.

My dad says, "On safari
you must wear a Tilley hat,"
which keeps him from perspiring
because he is too fat.

Some people who build houses
a hard hat they must wear
cause someone might drop something down
as you climb up a stair.

My hats are all so itchy
they won't stay on my head
they slip and slide and flop around
so that's why hats I dread.

HANDS

Oh wondrous hands!
Tracked by blue-veined rivers
with wrinkled knuckles
like moon craters
blotched and swollen.
A dry landscape.

Without you the flavour of comfort leaves.
Without your open palms of love, loneliness arrives.

You are supple dancers
over the dusty counters of life.
You wave love into air
and hang lines of words
out to dry.

Gestures are swaying grasses and flowers
drawing works of art
shadows on the walls of our souls.
You stroke away fear and pain
erasing stings, wrapping warmth into new life.

Oh wondrous hands!

THIS OLD GATE

Cobwebs hang on rotten vines
at the gate to our neighbour's house.
Tree falls blanketed with leaves
lie on the once worn path.
Only birds pass by
and a wild rabbit or two.

Now, doors are closed
where once a welcome mat
and a cup to share
made our laughter dance.

Words quickly said
our friendship fled
unforgiving we turned away
let our shared lives fall apart.

This gate too will one day crumble
and no one care
that once this was the way
to the home of a friend.

ASHES

These tall trees are now planks
in cabin walls eaten away by carpenter ants.
I hear them at night, gnawing, gnawing.
The cancer eats away at my tall, strong Dad.
His bones look through his skin at me
skin stretched like hide on a frame
the metal of his soul on fire.

The old stove eaten through
by burning salty wood
water tank rusty
chimney plugged and crumbling.
My Dad's throat stopped up too.
He cannot eat and smiles wearily
running his hand through grey hair
thick, like the moss on the cabin roof.

No cobwebs in his brain
but spiders decorate the magazines
and books his eyes absorbed.
Eyes that picked out a deer swimming at sea
he pointed.
I did not see.

He taught me about the stars
the plants, the world and ideas
stored now in tissue
under my skull.

His huge hands that lie curled in his lap
once lifted me high in the air
held my hands on walks
used an axe to split a log
stroked tears from my eyes.

When the moon rises through the dirty windows
I wonder how long will he see this?
How long will he stoke the old fire
or make porridge and
stumble into the woods, taking out the ashes?

Ashes.

TOM CAT

His Honda hums round the corner of the alley.
The tires claw for traction.

Leaping onto the deck, he hammers on the door
slides open the glass, and with whiskered smile
eyes gleaming says, *"Is Kelly here?"*

He glides silently through my kitchen,
leaps onto the sofa and flings off his helmet
shaking his long hair.

Later, at dinner, I notice a perpetual grin
as he picks delicately at the food
brushing whiskers with napkin.
Wordless, his eyes slide sideways to my daughter.

I imagine a tail
twitching
under the table.

Jan Bush

NIGHT PROWLER

Will-o-wisp of the windowsill
your wandering ways I know
winding your tail round a whiskered face
when it's three a.m. and I'm low.

Whack goes your paw on my cheekbone
lumped with the weight on my chest
and a purr as loud as thunder
interrupting my rest.

You clean your claws through the quilting
and lick on my open toes
then tickle my cheeks with your whiskers
and drool all over my nose.

Oh how can I sleep through this torment?
Oh why do you need me now?
Couldn't you wait until morning
when I spoon out my love with the chow?

CHILD'S PLAY

Earth

pulling moon

moon pulling the great tides

tides rising and falling creating winds

pulling colourful kite on a long string filling the sky.

At the end of the string a little girl

in a pink dress being pulled

earth pulling child

wind dying

kite falling

Child

S
I
G
H
I
N
G

CHRISTMAS IN TYROL

Our breath rises like dry-ice steam
rising...rising in frosted air
in the lift tram looking down
at a small village
ant people, gingerbread houses
white...white...white.
We sway to an abrupt stop
jump onto our skis
flying...flying
over snow hummocks, around trees
swirl to a stop at the bottom.

A one legged skier
fearlessly speeds toward us
hair flying, face flushed
smiling a frosty smile.

Into the village we glide
stop at the bakery
where skiers sit with
bright red faces
and chocolate moustaches.

Invited to city hall
we aliens sit among Austrians
drinking their beer.
The little mayor dressed
in leather pants, knee socks and boots
dances with a tall Canadian girl.

Staggering back to our hotel
we snuggle under downy quilts
dreaming of snowy heights.
At midnight we hear
alpine horns blow
and jump from our beds.

The church is alight
horses trotting, sporting bells
bringing muffled bodies
to the Christmas Eve service.

Freezing church
little girls, like angels,
in white chiffon
knees blue with cold
sing carols
facing a black shadowy altar
high in a balcony at the back
trumpets blow again.

After the service
outside in the town square
a huge bonfire reflects
flames against the buildings.
We all sing
until the fire sighs
and falling crystals
land in our eyes.
We blink away the magic.

ANIMAL EYES

She comes in from the woods
the beach and the river.
Her tangled hair filled with clover, burrs
flowers and salt.
Thoughtful eyes catch the sun
twinkle with sparks of water, fire...
animal eyes.

"A quiet one," I think,
as her delicate hands stroke the dog
carry a flower.
She sits for hours watching clouds.
Then...quicksilver
runs barefoot down the trail
through the woods.
"Look, look"... she says.
Absently I glance,
focus and see a tiny bee.

Even now
years later
she says, *"Look, look!"*...
But I am old and blind.

AT THE EDGE OF THE WOODS

Across the field at the edge of the woods
there's something hairy, something scary
watching with burning eyes through the gaps
from the shadows between the alders
and stretched fingers of cedar.

Dark and darker
body hunched there by the ferns
behind that stump.

My dog smells it.
His ridge stands up like a stickleback
his eyes fixed on the edge of the woods
his body freezes, one paw lifted.
There's a fetid rank smell
from the damp moss crushed and wounded
there at the edge of the woods.

There's a lurking beast there.
That thing at the edge of the woods
filling my mind with dread
waiting, waiting, waiting
at the edge of the woods.

ELK

Out of the dark forest
in morning mist,
ghostly monsters
slowly emerge.
Large racks swirl
waving the mist back.
I see them,
dark muzzles, light creamy backs
a target for poachers.

They are too big
to be ignored
this all male herd.

Prehistoric beasts
with huge hooves
legs like trees
immoveable.
A wall of bone and leather
leaving a heavy print in the mud.

A smaller elk challenges.
He whistles and charges
racks clack together.
The bigger elk pushes back
casually walks away.
Their world of trees, grass, shrubs
and river keeps them moving
through these mountains.

Before they leave
huge heads turn
to observe me.
I am small.
I am nothing in their world...

Except when I have a gun.

TWO SCENES

No slugs today,
only a snake smiling and
moving the grasses for my feet.

> In a far off world,
> only desert
> heat and insurrection.

Weeds grip the soil
making my body sweat.

> In the desert, anger
> the death of friends and enemies.

Light rain
touches the leaves of the lilac,
moves oregano to rouse my senses
wakes up the roses' aroma.

> A stench of death
> around the outposts,
> plastic explosives hidden
> in children's pack sacks.

At the end of the garden,
quiet waters flow to the sea
carrying fingerlings for the future.

> At the end of the world,
> angry political trainers
> teach children
> to hate enough to die.

Here a child hands me a flower.

OH CANADA

Oh Canada, lonely lady
sitting on the edge of an iceberg
warming your feet at the border
digging in your heels at your bossy neighbour
waving your tree-filled arms at the sky.

You breed poets, writers and artists
engineers, scientists, adventurers
who tumble down from your ancient waterfalls
out of your rocky heights.

Modest and unassuming
you hide your beauty in the mists of Niagara
waiting with open arms.
You were made tolerant by storm, ice and snow.
Your many bridegrooms in Ottawa
persuaded you to listen
but failed in their promises.
You heard their lies knowing they were too small
for such a big country.

Your cloak gilds prairie wheat fields in autumn
spreads green across Ontario in spring
whitens Nunavit in time for caribou herds to migrate.
Your patient tears flood rivers for salmon to spawn.
Your voice calls the swans back to the north.

You were formed long before you were peopled.
No footprint on your sandy shores
marked that ancient beginning.
Where then did you come from?
Waters receded, mountains erupted.
You were shaped, stretched into lakes,
streams, prairies and islands.
Canada, greed and avarice are at your door
...don't answer.

SISTERS

I float in the seas with my sisters
salt and blood so much the same
inside and out
the surge pulls us here and there
our hair floats
in curls, waves and braids.

Yet we sing in storm
we sing the songs of tides of life
we sing earth's song.

We long to return
to know magic
to know moons
to know the ancient ways of healing.

For this we weep in sun and rain
our tears are phosphorous
we laugh in storm and ride the surf
the wind at night sings the answers.

We float and listen
looking for signs
looking for prophecy.

No one on shore...knows how safe we are.

Jan Bush

Judith Heron knew she had a poet's heart as a young child. Being laughed at for "*making poems*" in grade three, she went underground only to resurface at university. There she could often be found writing in the Japanese Gardens rather than studying in the biology labs. As a young mother, she soothed her burning impulse to write by creating "little ditties" and putting Christina Rosetti poems to music for her children. She now has two grandchildren who show enthusiasm to hear their Grammy's stories; one even reports having her "*own songs in her tummy to tell.*"

Creative expression in the arts has progressively become the force of passion in Judith's life. Whether she creates with yarn, glass and stone, photography or poetic images, her focus is always on colour and hue, subtle nuances, and attention to the simplest details. She is intent on seeking out the Divine at the heart of every experience. In recent years poetry has become a favoured venue for celebrating a gentle faith in the resiliency of the human spirit.

Judith was born on the West Coast. She has lived in the Comox Valley, on Vancouver Island for over thirty years, where she is a well-loved and respected counselor in private practice. She is a passionate member of "Mostly Poets" and belongs to "A Circle of Writers".

TABLE OF CONTENTS

Feathers 129

Company We Keep 130

Straight Skirts 131

Only You 132

Mulching By Moonlight 133

Darkening Limbs 134

Keeping Pace With Time 135

Wayward Poet 136

Veil Of Tears 137

Myriad Shades Of Blue 138

Sorrow And Lace 139

Onions 140

Gazing 141

For My Sake 142

FEATHERS

under the bed
on top of the box
of hidden lace
and old tablecloths
my fingers find
a memory board
made years ago
for Aunt Vera who
by family standards
died young

the empty wooden frame
discovered among her things
hearts stenciled orange
in the corners
bits of broken mirror
old ceramic beads
her half finished silver rings
stoneless
as unfinished dreams

and a poem
which ended
"a kiss every night
on the top of my head"
placed beside some feathers...
small speckled feathers
of some unknown inland bird
caught in the bushes
gone skeleton
by the time
I found it

THE COMPANY WE KEEP

I like to be with women
who don't give two bits
for how I earn my living
or what I wear...
whose hair has been more
than generously sprinkled with grey
who understand
about leaving shoes at the door
and ask for slippers
so their feet won't get cold

I like to be with women
who don't get uptight
if someone or even most of us are late
who choose instead to be grateful
that everyone arrived
miss the one who didn't make it
because of grandchildren
and feel the poignant relief
that it was not a graver thing

I like to be with women
who are mostly interested
in the soundness of my mind
who hear my heart flutter in my words
women who offer critique
as kindly for another
as they wish it for themselves
and all our poems are better
for the company we keep

STRAIGHT SKIRTS...1959

forbidden
beyond question
an absolute *"no"*
only for the wretched
and the loose

how I squirrel'd away
my babysitting money
in quarters
saved up
for a yard of cloth
watched the older girls
get on and off
the school bus
buttocks pulsing
with mystery

then came
that inevitable day
Gail Byerki
from down the road
caught hitch-hiking
out in the valley
suddenly dead
tightest skirt of them all
whitest lips

when I finally
had the courage
to sew my first skirt
straight and tight
I put a small bow
above the kick pleat
to protect me...
to dare the darkness
not to follow

ONLY YOU
A eulogy

only you
would leave a bundle
of September basil
woven with a feather
on the chair
outside my window...
this image nestles
indelibly
among fragments
of memory

I know it will rest
beside a morning
decades past
shattered dreams ago...
sitting in bed
paisley all around me
our children playing
in a distant room...
your footstep
on the stairs...
the tray coming
around the corner
saffron and orange
nasturtiums
in a little cracked vase...
the tiniest glimpse
of something luscious...

for these important
things
you never used
words

MULCHING BY MOONLIGHT

it is the first of November
they say it will rain tomorrow
night's heavy frost has pulled
the last of autumn's colour to the ground

I come home at lunch
rake these golden remnants
into paths that lace across the lawn
lying pale as tattered prayer flags

I try to start the mower
morning chill has stilled the oil
I lug the machine up three steps
into my living room to warm

when I arrive home after dusk
my neighbour laughs
says I've *"found a lady's trick"*
I feel clever as the engine starts

chasing ribbons of leaves
around the grass
guided by memory...under a darkening sky
I am mulching by moonlight

meanwhile salmon splashing in the creek
at the bottom of the yard
are keeping their own appointment
with this season's pull

I smile at my own creative urgency

DARKENING LIMBS

darkening limbs
in November rain
strong against the grey
burgeoning creek

limbs I remember
you cherished
how deeply they bowed
so near the water

cedars on the bank
bend lower every winter
below silver salmon
still splash upstream

years ago we sat
at the window
silent at peace
seeing everything

when I knew
you were leaving
I did a cruel yet
necessary thing

I hauled your ladder
into the creek
rose on wobbly steps
to clasp a favorite limb

I raised the saw
and cut clear through
was soaked
as heaviness hurled below

I dragged the severed thing
sweated with each cut
threw bits
onto the burning pile

you would have seen it
I counted on that
one more thing
unspoken between us

I trick myself no longer
by saying "*it spared the fish*"
it was our bond
I was cutting through

so what remains...
only amends to the forest
for carrying the scar
of my unwanted parting

KEEPING PACE WITH TIME

stepping from the bath
without my glasses
into the cornflower blue light

towel swaddling me
against the new spring chill
I bend to pick something
up from the floor

folding over softened flesh
reaching
I discover
my dampened footprint

135

THE WAYWARD POET

tall enough to stoop
body bigger
than his soul can hold
gypsy vagabond
"hitchhiker"
from the edge
of somewhere
I have never been

long hair thrusting
from under a fleece toque
worn on this warm
June afternoon
sweatshirt hanging low
over baggy shorts
something Guatemalan
hard-worn footwear
yearning to return
to the beat
of the pavement

reading poetry
so keen so raw
my heart is seared
not wounded
wakened by the glory
of this creative pulse
which surely has saved
at least one life

" THE VEIL OF TEARS " *

sixty years of sorrow
five hundred years of rain
both pressed
by gravity down
upon the earth
within the layered
confines
of the heart

which is the more
miraculous
her tears at last
upon his quiet naked chest
or the ancient water spilling
over the mouth
of the cave

both so pure

*   Cave formation in
Zion National Park, Utah

Judith Heron

MYRIAD SHADES OF BLUE

the rain is dark
the hour suspended
somewhere before noon

the fire bursts
with dried cedar
my fingers smell of smoke

outside a rush of wind
pulls yellow magnolia leaves
graciously toward the ground

caught from the corner of my eye
they quiet the wooden knitting needles
now resting in my lap

the yarn
in myriad shades of blue
lies still

I draw this moment in
an extra thread...

SORROW AND LACE

I knit my love
in finest silk
over and over
between my fingers

lavender spirit
sweetest lace
how else can I say
"*I'll miss you*"

with each twist
of the yarn
the ball grows smaller
your life shorter

then comes the moment
to cast off
or keep knitting
I stare at the end

try to stop
the inevitable
from
happening

ONIONS

when I return from my Christmas journey
the car, the ferry, the high mountain passes
and the snow, the grandchildren...
I go to buy a few groceries
strain to remember what I need
carefully choose carrots for stew
fat onions since mine are gone
a little meat, proverbial milk and eggs

when I get home and open the cupboard
I find plenty of onions
still lying in their basket...
I have taken inventory
from my daughter's kitchen not mine
I have been in her world
entered it so entirely that I must
reorient to my own

this is not a bad thing
it is tender and sweet
like the handmade label
on her poultry seasoning
which has both
our names on it

GAZING

look into
the August sky
past twilight
and before dawn
if shooting stars
are what you long for

if it is the mystery
you seek
look into
the blackness
of February
eyelashes frosted
from staring
night after night
till finally
the calling of geese
shatters
all loneliness

FOR MY SAKE

there will come a season
when I am no more
do not put flowers at my door
do not search for reason

in the spring
take up an armful
of pussy willows
salmonberry, apple blossoms

put them on your table
take them to a neighbour
sprinkle petals
in the creek

in summer precious
peonies, roses
forget-me-nots
I am there

eat the sweet fruits
of the earth
let my ashes nourish
apricot and plum

wildly in the fields
along the roadside
let me be nowhere
in particular everywhere

let your hands
be stained from picking
eat ripe cherries
while standing on the fence

find pears, apples
dropping to the ground
found fruit
belongs to everyone

when the first snow falls
notice how crows persist
still talking to the sky
grateful for shelter

and so am I

Judith Heron

INDEX OF PREVIOUSLY PUBLISHED POEMS

Louie Adell:
"Chanukah Derailed" and "Chemainus" published in *Peer Glass*
Hudson Valley Writers' Guild, publisher. Albany N.Y. 2003

Marieluisa Auterson:
"God Is", "Dawn", "Plenty", "Conception", "Death", "Celebrating",
"Birth", published in *Path In Between,* Plateau Publishing,
Courtenay, 1994.
"Raised" (Cancer), in *Illness and the Healing Call of the Formative
Early Recollection,* paper presented at NASAP Convention 1997.
"Raised", "The Poem", "Birth" all published in *Illness seeking Healing
Within the Mind,* a video created by: Video Studio, Del Hansen, DVD,
2006.

Elizabeth Bartel:
"Lisa by the Pool," published in *Prairie Journal* #40
"Walking on the Estuary Path," published in *Prairie Journal #46*

Vera Jensen:
"Riches," published in *Glad Tidings* 1997, "Moonstalker," published
in *Canadian Writers' Journal* 1997, "Moon Song," published in *The
Plowman* 1997.
"Fish boat," published in *Island Guardian, 1997.*
"Who is that Old Woman" published in *Room of One's Own,* 1998.
"On Summer Days," published in *Retired Teachers Bulletin,* 2003
"Ordinary Women" published in *Ascent/aspirations,* 2006.

REORDER FORM

If you would like to purchase additional copies of

A MURDER OF CRONES – *A COLLECTION*
by the "MOSTLY POETS"

WRITE:

Mostly Poets
c/o Cape Lazo Studio
1123 Sand Pines Crescent
Comox, B.C.
V9N 3V3

EMAIL:

capelazostudio@gmail.com